Stepping Out *on* FAITH

Shirley A. Spann

Deluxe Publications

First printing, January 1992

Scripture quotations are taken from the *Holy Bible,* King James version.

Deluxe Publications
P. O. Box 740
Boston, Massachusetts 02112
(617) 825–4388

Printed in the United States of America.

ISBN–0–9632239–0–9

This book is dedicated to my mother

Arlene Spann-Gooding

Thank you for your love, support, and encouragement, and for being a constant inspiration to me and teaching me how to keep "the faith."

This book is also dedicated in loving memory to two people who have exemplified and lived by faith and taught me to do the same: my grandmother, Carrie F. Spann, and my pastor and Bible study teacher, Reverend James H. Holland, Jr.

Finally, to all of those individuals who have goals that they would like to achieve, this book is also dedicated to you.

Contents

Acknowledgments

Many thanks are extended to all who have helped to make this book possible.

A special word of thanks to Rev. Dr. Kirk B. Jones for writing the Foreword to this book.

Foreword

Stepping Out on Faith is like the early Christian letters written by the Apostle Paul and others: a testament to the presence and power of God in everyday life. Those first Christian writers wrote in gratitude for the blessings of God in their own lives and in anticipation of God blessing many others through the reading of their works. In like manner, Miss Spann's book is both an act of worship and evangelism.

To read her work is to see that there exists a God of great power and love Who wishes to be involved in the living of our days. We ignore the involvement of God in our lives to our own detriment. To the extent that we embrace our God, we rise to the high level of abundance and excellence in life that God intends for us all.

Along the path of this book are two "nuggets" that the mature believer does well to hold close to his heart. The first is that faith and work go hand and hand. To pray and not work toward God's will is not to really pray. The second is that Jesus' religion is social as well as personal religion. God's will is known, experienced, and celebrated in association with our brothers and sisters in and outside our respective families and congregations.

Very shortly, you will be blessed by words that will remind you or maybe tell you for the very first time that God made you, loves you, and has a special plan for your life. Give your life to Him; you will never be the same ever again!

The Rev. Dr. Kirk Byron Jones,
Pastor, Ebenezer Baptist Church, Boston, Massachusetts
Adjunct Professor, Religion and Society
Andover Newton Theological School
Newton Centre, Massachusetts

1

Introduction

In the privacy of my home, I can vividly recall writing: *"Dear Lord, thank you for everything that you have done for me."* With a heart filled with adoration and thanks, I wrote these words as an opening for many of the letters I wrote to the Lord when I was a child. I always believed that God was all–powerful and that He was able to help us achieve anything we asked of Him.

Over the years as I acquired more knowledge about Him and accepted Jesus Christ as my Saviour, I watched my faith in Him increase and watched him perform wondrously in my behalf, enabling me to reach specific goals. God is just, and He can also help you achieve your goals if you have faith in Him.

However, faith cannot stand alone. Too often many of us petition the Lord to supply a specific need, sit back comfortably, and wait for Him to answer without doing any work to allow it to transpire.

Goals are meant to be achieved. To achieve them, you must have faith and work simultaneously. Throughout this book, *Stepping Out on Faith*, I emphasize that faith without work is dead. Faith must always be accompanied by work. We must do those things necessary to accomplish each task as we believe the Lord to grant us our desires.

Consequently, in addition to the unbeatable combination of faith and work, the Lord's granting of our requests or desires is predicated upon our obedience to Him. We must do what the Lord tells us, making His command our goal and being careful not to disobey Him.

There are numerous reasons why we disobey God when we fail to do what we feel He wants us to do. Fear of failure, doubt, and procrastination are just a few scapegoats that we frequently use as refuge. Yet, we often forget that there is no hiding from the omniscient God.

The only fear that is permissible by God is to fear Him. Yet, the fear of failure is commonplace with many of us; sometimes we are reluctant to initiate our goals whenever we sense the slightest possibility of failure. The mere thought of its consequences, which we usually view negatively, causes us to remain idle and not take any action to achieve what we want.

A noted talk show host once stated, "I have never had great failures—only great lessons." Her statement is one that we can benefit from: to learn something from every situation that we are quick to deem as a failure.

Consequently, the worst kind of failure is the failure to try. When we fail to try, we eliminate any chance of knowing whether we would have failed or succeeded. Instead of trying and risking failure, we proceed with our lives in other situations that provide more comfort.

While the fear of failure is one roadblock that prevents us from forging ahead to achieve our goals, we can also doubt our abilities to actualize those goals. Doubt then paralyzes and immobilizes us within its stronghold. Amid the paralysis, we can also doubt whether the goal is one from God and may become very reluctant to initiate any plan to achieve it.

Reluctance in this manner can be well taken, but sometimes it can become just another excuse to remain idle. In this case, we want the Lord to tell us repeatedly what He wants us to do. However, once you are convinced that God is the One giving instructions, why pretend you need further assurance?

Remember, you cannot fool God, for He is omniscient, and He knows when you are unwilling to do His work. When He realizes that you are not inclined to undertake His command, He finds an obedient soul who wants to labor for Him and commissions that person to fulfill His desire. He does not, however, withdraw His command from you in your disobedience. Your disobedience to God is punishable.

While His capacity to punish is evidenced throughout the *Holy Bible,* procrastination can also cause us to shun a task, causing disobedience to God. Procrastination is an evil and becomes one of our biggest enemies when we have a task to accomplish. It prohibits us from making the start that is necessary to achieve our goals.

With procrastinators, the time is never the present time. Another time is always a better time to start. "I'll do it later." Again, for those who are considered chronic procrastinators, later never comes.

In its evil disguise as comfort, procrastination can stem from fear of facing the unknown. The uncertainty of what may occur can cause the procrastinator to make a habit of putting off making any effort to realize his goal.

While many of us may have our distinct reasons for procrastinating, the question remains: Why put off a task that you feel the Lord wants you to do? Be obedient, for with God, obedience brings great rewards.

Whether it is fear of failure, doubt, or procrastination that is keeping you idle and causing you to shun your goal, I pray that you move beyond that roadblock. Step out on your faith in God to achieve the task or goal that you feel He has given you.

Stepping out on faith simply means making an effort to achieve your goal while believing that God, our Higher Power, will help you as you try to help yourself. You can obtain His help by believing in His Son, Jesus Christ.

With Christ, all things are possible. With Him on your side, you don't have to worry or spend sleepless nights wondering what lies ahead. Instead, you begin to acknowledge that whatever unforeseen or difficult situation concerning your goal lies ahead, it is never too difficult for God to perform. You maximize your potentials and can help more people when you believe that nothing is impossible with Christ.

As you try to reach your goal, you must have faith in God. Chapter 2 of this book discusses faith (increasing it and allowing it to work for you).

Chapter 3 discusses that when God inspires you to achieve a goal, the primary reason is to bring honor and glory to His name and to become a blessing for others. It is my belief, too, that a goal inspired by God can also be affirmed through prayers.

Chapter 4 reminds you that before you try to step out to reach your objective, you should not forget to pray. Prayer is essential to your walk with God and opens your communication with Him. It keeps you aligned with His will and also shows that you are counting on Him (and only Him) to lead you.

Chapter 5 emphasizes that once you have prayed about your goal in faith and are convinced that God is giving you the task, you must believe in yourself. Maintain a positive attitude toward achieving what you have set out to do. Have confidence in your God–given abilities, and learn how to accept criticism.

It is highly unlikely that you will succeed at your goal without being confronted by critics who may not want you to accomplish your task. Be ready for them, and gird yourself with unmovable faith in God. Strong faith helps you to withstand any test and overcome any criticism.

Unfortunately, no matter how hard you try to do what you feel is right, problems can still arise. Chapter 6 explains that despite how tough a situation seems, there is nothing too difficult for God. He can make a way for you to achieve your goal.

Chapter 7 discusses that you should always seek to please God with what you are trying to achieve. Always put God first, for when this earthly tabernacle is dissolved, only what you do for the Lord will stand.

As you turn each page, I pray that you become more and more inspired to achieve all of your goals. God emphasizes in His Word that you are more than a conqueror. If He says that you can do all things through Christ, you can! Have faith.

2

Having Faith in God

"And Jesus answering saith unto them, Have faith in God" (Mark 11:22).

You have probably heard at least one of these statements about faith: "You can do it if you have the faith to believe;" "Faith will move mountains for you;" or "You need a little faith." Perhaps you have been asked: "Where is your faith?"

"And Jesus answering saith unto them, Have faith in God" (Mark 11:22). What is faith? Are you faithful or faithless?

Acquire a clear understanding of faith so you can exercise it properly in your life. Unfortunately, many people profess faith but in the wrong things, putting their faith and trust in power, popularity, money, security, and man.

Some people even put their initial faith in doctors, not acknowledging that it is the Lord Who works through them to bring about healing. However, some doctors have much faith and are quick to acknowledge God's power to heal—faithful men indeed.

Most unfortunate of all is when we do not put our faith in man, we sometimes have the conviction that there is no such thing as faith. However, because of His great love for us, God has given us a worthy faith to live by: Jesus Christ, faith at its greatest. Power, popularity, money, and security are temporal, but Jesus Christ, Who has power to give us all things to enjoy, is everlasting.

If faith achieves all that so many people claim that it does, we should be highly faithful. In addition, it is imperative that we are faithful, for it is the only way that we can ever please God.

It is your faith that really moves God, allowing you to reach your goals. Know more about faith and what it can do. You can also increase your faith through the study of God's Word.

What Is Faith

Faith is the act of believing. In the spiritual realm, upon which this book primarily focuses, faith means believing in God and His power to work for you.

To receive all of the blessings of faith, you must believe in God, "for he that cometh to God must believe that he is, and that he is a rewarder of them that diligently seek him" (Heb. 11:6). You must believe that He exists. "The fool hath said in his heart, There is no God" (Psalm 53:1).

Don't be like the foolish; everything that exists is evidence of God's existence, for "All things were made by him; and without him not any thing made that was made" (John 1:3). In essence, the Creator of the heaven and the earth and everything therein is God, the Word.

The *Holy Bible* also states that "the Word was made flesh, and dwelt among us" (John 1:14). Here the Scripture writer is referring to God's Son, Jesus Christ, Whom God sent on earth to save us from our sins.

"For God so loved the world, that he gave his only begotten Son, that whosoever believeth in him should not perish, but have everlasting life" (John 3:16). Because of man's sinful nature, the only way that he can commune with God is through His Son. Jesus Christ Himself said: "I am the way, the truth, and the life: no man cometh unto the Father, but by me" (John 14:6). If you want God to grant you your desire, you must ask Him in Jesus' name. Jesus Christ is your way to God.

If you believe in God and His Son, believe also in the Holy Ghost, for we serve a triune God: Father, Son, and Holy Ghost, Who are One. The Holy Spirit can lead and guide you in your endeavor and help you along your way.

The Holy Spirit is the great Teacher and Revealer. He can teach you things that you may have thought was too complex to understand. The Holy Spirit can also reveal to you things to come. Foremost, He is your Comforter.

Before Jesus' death, He assured His disciples that He would not leave them comfortless. "But the Comforter, which is the Holy Ghost, whom the Father will send in my name, he shall teach you all things, and bring all things to your remembrance, whatsoever I have said unto you" (John 14:26).

If you have not accepted the Lord, Jesus Christ, as your personal Saviour, do it today. If you want the Holy Spirit to dwell within you, ask. God will give the "Holy Spirit to them that ask him" (Luke 11:13). These actions require faith, which returns us to our initial question: What is faith?

> Unfortunately, many people profess faith but in the wrong things, putting their faith and trust in power, popularity, money, security, and man.

A very familiar and often quoted definition of faith found in the *Holy Bible* states, "Now faith is the substance of things hoped for, the evidence of things not seen" (Hebrews 11:1). Your unshakable belief (or faith) is what produces the things that you are hoping for or want to occur. It is believing that God will bring to pass what you ask of Him without any evidence or sign of how He will cause it to happen.

Believing in your heart that somehow something is going to happen is all that faith requires. When you feel that you must see to believe, then you are faithless. Faith elevates you beyond what your eyes can see and what your mind can comprehend and allows you to acknowledge that God has the power to do all things.

One day I was desperate to reach the post office before it closed because I was informed of an important piece of mail. It was 4:15 P.M. and the post office's closing hour was 5:00 P.M. From where I was located, I knew that my commute would be 1–hour long, and I would probably arrive after the post office had closed. However, I kept praying and believing along the way that someone would let me into the post office.

Just as I had thought, when I arrived, it was after 5:00 P.M. The security guard came to the door and told me that he could not let me in. Despite how much I pleaded with him, he just wouldn't let me in and walked away from the door.

Other people who needed postal services also came by and saw that the office was closed and just walked away—exactly what anyone would have done. But no, not Shirley. I had faith that someone would let me into that post office.

I knocked on the door, looked in, and saw another postal worker busily working. Strangely enough, I kept standing at the door as though I knew that he or someone else would open it.

Finally, my moment of victory arrived. The postal worker waved at me, telling me to remain at the door until the security guard come to open it. Well, I did and was able to pick up my piece of mail. When you truly believe that something is going to happen, it causes it to transpire.

My reflection upon this experience is not to convey disrespect for man's policies, but they *are* man–made, and God can move beyond them. God is sovereign and can do whatever He wants to do when He wants to. He has opened jail doors, shut the mouths of lions, and performed many other acts that show His awesome sovereignty.

Believe that you can achieve your goal, and God can make it come to pass by His Spirit, for He is a Spirit. "Not by might, nor by power, but by my spirit, saith the Lord of hosts" (Zech. 4:6). It is by His Spirit that He moves in your behalf, enabling you to achieve your endeavor.

Unfortunately, many of us expect immediate responses from God. If He does not act upon our requests or petitions when we want Him to, we allow doubt to surface. We wonder whether He has heard our plea or if He is going to grant us our desires at all.

You must be fully convinced that God will supply your needs through Christ despite the amount of time that elapses before He delivers. Remain faithful and witness the Lord's moving by His power to help you achieve your goal. But how much faith do you need?

The *Holy Bible* talks about having "little" and "much" faith. Jesus tells us that all we need is faith the size of a mustard seed to do great things. Now, this is very small faith—minute, indeed, especially to accomplish large feats. On the other hand, He also mentions that we need much faith.

"Because of your unbelief: for verily I say unto you, If ye have faith as a grain of mustard seed, ye shall say unto this mountain, Remove hence to yonder place; and it shall remove; and nothing shall be impossible unto you" (Matt. 17:20). He explains that even with small faith, great and mighty things can happen.

Implying that much faith is needed, He speaks, "O ye of little faith" (Matt. 16:8). Here He implies that you need more than a little faith; sometimes great faith is required to grasp His power.

In light of these Scriptures, I believe that Jesus does not want us to become entangled in arguments of the exact amounts of faith we should have in any given situation. Ask the Lord in prayer for adequate faith in each situation to reach His powers, and He can grant you faith according to His will.

He can increase your faith and remove all doubts for what you are trying to accomplish.

Increase Your Faith

Faith is paramount and also a prerequisite before you can ask anything of God. You can increase your faith in Him through the study of the *Holy Bible* and prayer.

The *Holy Bible* is God's infallible inspired words, revealing our past, present, and future. It holds sacred records of all the great works that God performed through those who believed in Him in Biblical times.

I find that the more I study His Word and read beautiful stories about people such as Noah, Daniel, King David, Moses, Abraham, Elijah, and Jesus that truly highlight God's power, the more my faith in God increases.

Reading of the wonders that He has performed for His people makes me believe that He can do the same for me. "Of a truth I perceive that God is no respecter of persons" (Acts 10:34). He does not discriminate amongst His children. But He requires you to make Him your first priority, allowing Him to become your first love and desire.

When you love someone, you want to know as much as possible about that person. To know more about God is to study His Word.

In one of the Apostle Paul's epistles, he states that we should: "Study to shew thyself approved unto God, a workman that needeth not to be ashamed, rightly dividing the word of truth" (II Tim. 2:15).

When you study His Word, not only are you increasing your faith in God, but you are also showing yourself approved by Him, doing something that is pleasing in His sight. In addition, you will find that He has included everything in the *Holy Bible* that He wants you to know that is necessary concerning your Christian life.

Some people "have a zeal of God, but not according to knowledge" (Rom. 10:2). Your ardent interest in God is good, but not sufficient. Take time to learn about Him so that you can know how He wants you to live. In addition, you won't try to formulate your own rules of righteousness.

"For they being ignorant of God's righteousness, and going about to establish their own righteousness, have not submitted themselves unto the righteousness of God" (Rom. 10:3).

If you don't know what is right by God, how can you submit yourself to His righteousness? Sometimes we are quick to petition God for "any and everything," forgetting that He only hears us when we live righteously.

When you read the *Holy Bible,* you will begin to learn of His righteousness. In our Christian walk, we should not be so eager to accept another person's word on what the Lord requires, which can be very tempting. Know God and His laws for yourself, for you have to give an account to Him for all things that you do, righteous and unrighteous.

"Let the word of Christ dwell in you richly in all wisdom" (Col. 3:16). Don't study just for the sake of studying or just to let others know how much you know about the *Holy Bible*. This is hypocritical.

Let God's Word come into your heart and be evidenced in your life by the way that you live. When you do, He will grant you your desires.

Studying God's Word increases your faith in Him. Your faith can allow amazing things to happen to you.

Faith in Action

Activate your faith in God. Faith can propel you to accomplish what you are inspired to do, not knowing whether you are going to fail or succeed, for "according to your faith be it unto you."

If you believe you will fail, then await your failure, for it will surely come. Believe you will succeed through Christ, and you will, for there is no failure in Him.

As mentioned earlier, faith alone is not sufficient to produce results and must be accompanied by your works, for "faith without works is dead" (James 2:20). Work to prove your faith before God.

Hebrews, Chapter 11, gives us a summary of some of God's people, who had tremendous faith in Him and were also justified by their works. Take some time to read it, for your faith will also be justified by your work or action, doing whatever is necessary to hep you achieve your goal.

If you believe you will fail, then await your failure, for it will surely come. Believe you will succeed through Christ, and you will.

If you don't do anything to indicate that you have faith, where is your justification? Work hard, if necessary, to achieve your goal. If this requires putting a plan together, working more with others, and so forth, do so and put your faith to work.

A person cited in the *Holy Bible* most often for his faith is Abraham. Learn from his example and others mentioned in this chapter. Their stories help convey the power of faith.

Abraham was faithful to God and was ready and willing to sacrifice his only son. God, being so loving, did not allow Abraham to complete the sacrifice, but used it as a test of his faith.

God, seeing his faithfulness, sent an angel to Abraham to tell him how He was going to bless him. The blessing would be a reward for Abraham's faith that he had shown toward God.

"That in blessing I will bless thee, and in multiplying I will multiply thy seed as the stars of the heaven, and as the sand which is upon the sea shore; and thy seed shall possess the gate of his enemies; And in thy seed shall all the nations of the earth be blessed; because thou hast obeyed my voice" (Gen. 22:17–18).

We know that this great blessing came through Jesus Christ, in Whom all nations can be blessed, if they believe in Him.

Although God did not test Solomon as He did Abraham, Solomon exhibited great faith in God before his fall. Solomon was King David's son and also the third king to rule over Israel. God appeared to Solomon in a dream and told him, "Ask what I shall give thee."

Solomon knew the great task placed before him as a new king, and he wanted to judge the people fairly and righteously. His faith in God that He would grant his request led Solomon to respond, "Give therefore thy servant an understanding heart to judge thy people, that I may discern between good and bad" (I Kings 3:9).

Solomon's unselfish petition pleased God so much that He made him one of the wisest and richest men to ever walk on earth. When God appeared to Solomon in his dream, Solomon didn't have to believe that God was going to do what He said he would, but he believed, and God performed miraculously for him.

Another act of faith in action is that of the woman with the blood disease and how she believed that the Lord would heal her. It was her faith that convinced her that she would be healed of her affliction, if she could just touch the hem of Jesus' garment.

In the crowd, the woman managed to reach out and touch His garment, and Jesus said to her: "Daughter, be of good comfort; thy faith hath made thee whole." Because of her faith, she was healed.

Two blind men stepped out on faith when they cried out to the Lord to restore their sight, but Jesus asked them if they believed that He had power to heal, and they responded: "Yea, Lord."

Again, we, too, must believe that the Lord has power to perform what we ask of Him. When we do, and feel that the Lord is asking us the same question, respond in like manner: "Yea, Lord." Many times I find myself saying, "Lord, I know that You can do it, for I believe You have the power to do all things."

You must have faith in the Lord with no unbelief, a faith that does not waver. Therefore, rid yourself of all doubts. Unbelief was one of the prime hindrances in the Lord's ministry, especially in His own home town. It is said that He could do no great work there because of the people's unbelief.

To the people of His town, Jesus was just "another" person. Nevertheless, He did not abandon His Father's work. In other cities, He continued to teach His disciples, two of whom were Peter and John, who were very faithful men.

When Peter and John went up to the temple to pray, there was a man there who had never even walked. He was lame from birth and had to be carried to the temple gates.

One day when the man asked for alms as Peter was passing by, Peter said to him, "Silver and gold have I none; but such as I have give I thee: In the name of Jesus Christ of Nazareth rise up and walk" (Acts 3:6).

Peter had tremendous faith that the Lord could heal the lame man. "And he took him by the right hand, and lifted him up: and immediately his feet and ankle bones received strength. And he leaping up stood, and walked, and entered with them into the temple, walking, and leaping, and praising God. And all the people saw him walking and praising God" (Acts 3:7–9).

Peter later told the unbelievers that it was the lame man's faith that enabled him to walk. Likewise, it is your faith that enables you to reach your goal.

These are just some of the beautiful stories of faith in action illustrated in the *Holy Bible*. Your unwavering faith, coupled with your work, is your key to unlock any door.

3

Inspired by God

"For it is God which worketh in you both to will and to do of his good pleasure" (Phil. 2:13).

Our minds are often filled with innumerable thoughts and ideas. When we strive to walk close to God, He inspires within us thoughts and ideas to achieve specific goals that ultimately bring glory and honor to His holy name.

"For it is God which worketh in you both to will and to do of his good pleasure" (Phil. 2:13). We are God's creation—created for His good pleasure, working through us those things that are pleasing in His sight.

However pleasurable to Him, God knows His will for each one of us and can make it known to us in many different ways. Whether we are instructed or commissioned through a dream, vision, meditation, or through any other means to fulfill His desire, I believe that the Lord wants us to make that task our primary goal in life, relinquishing all others.

Reaching that goal may mean that we must work diligently and relentlessly toward achieving its successful end. In essence, step out on faith to achieve all that you feel God is inspiring you to do.

On the other hand, on the slightest occasion when we begin to stray away from our walk with God, Satan has his way of trying to fill our minds with unrighteous and evil thoughts in his attempt to cause us to disobey God. Satan is our enemy and uses this weapon to tempt us to do evil to glorify, honor, and magnify him.

Aren't you glad to know that the Spirit of the Lord is supreme and omnipotent and can crush and destroy the enemy's power?

Jesus reminded His disciples of this fact and told them, "I beheld Satan as lightning fall from heaven. Behold, I give unto you power to tread on serpents and scorpions, and over all the power of the enemy: and nothing shall by any means hurt you" (Luke 10:18–19).

As His disciples also, He gives us power to overcome evil in any form and wants us to think as He would. Once He fills us with His Holy Spirit, our thoughts become as His, filled with His love. The Apostle Paul encourages us to "Let this mind be in you, which was also in Christ Jesus" (Phil. 2:5).

If we pray and ask the Lord to give us His mind so that we can think as He would in all situations, He is faithful and just to fulfill our request. Otherwise, we cannot say that what enters our minds is heavenly inspired.

Since we know that not every thought that enters our minds is from God, we should be careful in our reaction to each thought. For example, if someone mistreats you or harms you maliciously, an immediate thought or response may be to do likewise to the offender.

That immediate thought on how to react is certainly not of the Lord. By being calm and remembering that you must try to live in accordance with God's Word, another thought encourages you to show love instead of hate.

Thinking as Jesus would, you know that you should: "Love your enemies, bless them that curse you, do good to them that hate you, and pray for them which despitefully use you, and persecute you" (Matt. 5:44).

As illustrated in the Scripture, God is good and merciful. It is not within His will that you do harm for harm but to love, bless, do good, and pray. This is the kind of God that we serve: good, righteous, and merciful.

When we live and love like the Lord wants us to, thoughts that enter our minds should not be so questionable. When you find yourself questioning whether a goal you are inspired to achieve is inspired by God, ask yourself:

"Does the goal bring honor and glory to God?"

"Does the goal bless others?"

"Is the goal affirmed through prayers?"

Honor and Glory to God

Do all things as unto God, showing Him merited respect and recognizing Him for being the Great I AM. Our actions, in words or deeds, should be performed and accompanied with marks of honor and glory to God.

We are to glorify God at all times. If what you feel you are inspired to achieve is contrary to His glorification, stop and pray for redirection. When you do, you will find yourself desiring to do something good, glorifying and honoring God.

We know that all good things come from our heavenly Father, and He works all things after the counsel of His own will. "We are his workmanship, created in Christ Jesus unto good works" (Eph. 2:10).

The Lord created us remarkably, and He wants us to do good works. Perhaps your work is to teach or preach His Truth or to allow Him to use you to heal the sick. What about the homeless and the poor?

The Lord may want you to reach out to help those who are incapable of helping themselves by inspiring you to open a food or clothing shelter. Maybe He wants you to implement some type of business or institution.

Our actions, in words or deeds, should be performed and accompanied with marks of honor and glory to God.

No one knows better than you what good work the Lord wants to do through you for His glorification. He may reveal to others what He wants you to do, but He never leaves you unknowing.

Whatever goal or dream you feel that He is inspiring in you, you are to use it, laboring in His vineyard. That goal is your tool *(or gift)* to be an instrument to help others, which ultimately glorifies God.

Wishing to possess another person's gifts is of no avail. He uses us in many different ways to get His work done. With God, there are differences of administrations and there are diversities of operations, "but it is the same God which worketh all in all" (I Cor. 12:6).

Therefore, don't be envious of another person's gifts, for He looks down on His entire vineyard and gives to you according to His will. Does everyone possess the same gift or perform the same task? No, and He doesn't intend for it to be done that way, "dividing to every man severally as He wills."

However, the Lord wants us to work together, cooperating with each other and have the same care for one another. If God has not anointed you to perform the same work that He has anointed someone else to do, don't try to dishonor the other person's work. Instead, pray and ask God to show you how you can work cooperatively with all of His laborers, "for we are all workers together with God."

Whatever work He wants you to do, He is not going to isolate you to allow you to perform it. The goal that He wants to work through you becomes a part of the light that He wants you to be for others.

Therefore, work in the midst of the people and do what He tells you to do, becoming a light to the world. Jesus says, "Let your light so shine before men, that they may see your good works, and glorify your Father which is in heaven" (Matt. 5:16).

If the Lord has inspired or entrusted you with a certain task, you have your specific work for His glorification. The more you obey Him the more He will bless you as you complete His work. Know, too, that your labor does not go unrewarded, for He is not unrighteous to forget the work that you labored. In addition, your labor will not be in vain, for He uses it to bless others.

Blessings for Others

If your desire is inspired by God, He is going to use it to bless others. He wants you to be "rich in good works, ready to distribute, willing to communicate" (I Tim. 6:18) or give to the needy.

If you feel that your blessings or possessions belong to you only, you are denying the basic goal that God has set for all men. Your giving of yourself allows God to reveal one of the true meanings of life. Therefore, never tire in giving and sharing or try to hinder someone else from doing his work.

If your goal is a hindrance to others, it is unlikely that your goal is of God, for God wants you to love and care for others. With Satan, he has his followers to believe that everyone should be for himself—self is emphasized.

With God, self is crucified, and His believers begin to say, "For God I live, and for God, I'll die." Living for God is loving and caring for one another, sharing and bearing each other's burdens, and keeping busy working to spread and promote the gospel.

Do you ever find yourself preoccupied with your own affairs, becoming too busy for others? If you do, think about altering your behavioral pattern to include helping others. However, there is no guarantee that the recipients of your philanthropic gestures will always appreciate them.

Nevertheless, be obedient and fulfill your Christian duty to do as the Scripture says: "Look not every man on his own things, but every man also on the things of others" (Phil. 2:4).

The Apostle Paul admonishes us with the Scripture, for he knew that the Lord wants each one of us to love and help one another with our blessings. Despite how little you may feel you have, the Lord wants you to share it with another, for there is always someone who is worse off than you.

Make giving of yourself a priority. "Give, and it shall be given you; good measure, pressed down, and shaken together, and running over, shall men give into your bosom. For with the same measure that ye mete withal it shall be measured to you again" (Luke 6:38).

In your giving, God can return to you exceedingly above what you have given away. When you are faithful over just a few, He says to you, "Well done, thou good and faithful servant: thou hast been faithful over a few things, I will make thee ruler over many things: enter thou into the joy of thy lord" (Matt. 25:21).

If your desire is inspired by God, He is going to use it to bless others.

We should be careful not to try to retain blessings that God gives us. In the second advent of the Lord, He is going to judge us for what we have done for our fellow man and bless us accordingly.

Wouldn't you want to be among those who the Lord tells: "Come, ye blessed of my Father, inherit the kingdom prepared for you from the foundation of the world: For I was an hungered, and ye gave me meat: I was thirsty, and ye gave me drink: I was a stranger, and ye took me in: Naked, and ye clothed me: I was sick, and ye visited me: I was in prison, and ye came unto me" (Matt. 25:34–36).

If God is inspiring you to do a particular work, obey Him for His glorification. He will do a good work through you to help another. Needless to say, you cannot help anyone if the Lord doesn't first place you in a position to be of service to another. Therefore, be thankful for what He has given you and be ready and willing to share.

All of our endeavors should honor and glorify God. If what you are trying to accomplish does not impact others positively, continue to pray and ask the Lord if your desire is of Him. God can affirm your desire through prayer.

4

Praying About Your Goal

"Be careful for nothing; but in every thing by prayer and supplication with thanksgiving let your requests be made known unto God" (Phil. 4:6).

Prayer, who can deny its amazing powers? Prayer is our gateway to God, Who holds all powers in His hands. All exercises in which the soul gives up self and clings to Christ are uttered in prayer. You need His power to enable you to achieve your goal.

If you love God and desire to achieve the goal that you feel He wants you to achieve, converse with Him as often as possible in prayer. Prayer is man's turning to God and God answering man. Turn to Him so that He can guide you as you climb to reach your goal.

After turning to Him, He can provide answers to any situation that is confronting you. Through prayer, you are guided sustained, nourished, directed, and comforted by the Holy Spirit. Whether you need blessings regarding finance, home, marriage, or healing, prayer is the answer. God has the power to bless you, but first, you must pray.

If you neglect to pray about what you are inspired to do, relinquish any thought of initiating it. If you attempt to start any endeavor without consulting God through prayer, it can be disastrous. Despite how successful something may appear in the beginning, if God is not in the midst of it, it will "come to naught." Stay close to God in prayer if you want to succeed.

Through prayer, the Lord can affirm your goal then lead you with His guidance. Getting guidance and direction from Him is the best decision you can ever make while trying to move ahead.

Know how to go before the Lord in prayer. All of your prayers should be done in faith. A prayer without faith is likened unto absent prayer. When you pray in faith, the Lord performs wondrous acts in your behalf.

Affirmation Through Prayer

God can make you to know whether or not He wants you to perform a particular task; He can affirm that desire. As He affirms the desire, you may think that what He is inspiring you to do is too difficult or strange. You may even think for a moment: "Surely, He doesn't mean me." Make no mistake by trying to disobey Him.

Pray that the Holy Spirit teaches you how to be obedient. It is crucial that you obey the Lord, despite how much you feel that His will may be extraordinary. "For who hath resisted his will? Nay but, O man, who art thou that repliest against God" (Rom. 9:19–20)? Who are you to say whether you should or should not obey the Lord? Aren't you the creation and He the Creator?

For your affirmation, you can even ask the Lord for a sign to assure you of His desire. This reminds me of the story of Gideon in the *Holy Bible*.

> If you love God and desire to achieve the goal that you feel He wants you to achieve, converse with Him as often as possible in prayer.

Gideon was a judge, whom God used to deliver His people from the Midianites, the Israelites' enemies. However, before God used Gideon to deliver the Israelites, Gideon thought that God was asking too much of him.

"Oh, my Lord, wherewith shall I save Israel? behold, my family is poor in Manasseh, and I am the least in my father's house" (Judges 6:15). It does not matter whether you are rich or poor. If God wants to achieve a task through you, He can do so.

Although Gideon felt that he was unworthy to fulfill God's desire, God did not withdraw His command. He told Gideon that He would be with him. Still, Gideon felt that he needed a sign for assurance. Because of this, God gave Gideon several signs and eventually used him to accomplish the task that He had set before him.

God can do the same with you to let you know His desire. After He affirms your task, be obedient to achieve it, for Jesus Christ Himself was obedient to His Father.

"Though he were a Son, yet learned he obedience by the things which he suffered" (Heb. 5:8).

In your obedience, remember to pray for guidance.

Seek the Lord's Guidance

Seek the Lord's guidance through prayer in everything that you aspire to achieve. He can direct your life through the Holy Spirit by leading you to specific Bible Scriptures and others that can help you. He can also guide you through your daily circumstances. You may wonder why certain things are happening to you and not to others or why you must endure certain hardships or incredible experiences.

Rest assured, for only the Lord knows, and He may be preparing you for what He knows that you must encounter down the road. Find comfort in a songwriter's words: "You'll understand it better by and by." Believe those words, for the Lord enables you to understand everything concerning your goal when you stay close to Him in prayer.

You shouldn't fear to utter any concern to the Lord in your prayer. He is there to help you and wants you to come to Him. In His Word, He warns and encourages us to: "Be careful for nothing; but in every thing by prayer and supplication with thanksgiving let your requests be made known unto God" (Phil. 4:6). He is all–knowing and knows what you want to talk about before you open your mouth, yet prayer is still essential.

Pour out your heart to God in prayer. As you talk to Him, you can talk to Him as you would a friend, although He is a Spirit. No matter how big or small the situation may be, talk to the Lord and seek His counsel.

He is our Great Counsellor and wants us to seek Him for advice. His counsel guides us in directions that we must take in order to reach our goals. The Lord also has a miraculous way of putting others in our paths to aid us. Go to Him first.

If you fail to go directly to Him, you increase your chance of being confronted by others who feel that they know the right way or right approach for you to follow. If you are not careful, you can suddenly find yourself adhering to plans that were devised by others and behaving as they dictate. Be careful!

Believe me, if you cannot get an answer from the Lord, you won't be able to get an answer from anywhere else; go to God first. Although your answer may come through someone else, you should go to God first. Surely, His counsel is true and final, and you should shun advice from those who do not fear Him. When you avoid ungodly counsel, consider yourself blessed. For He says in His Word, "Blessed is the man that walketh not in the counsel of the ungodly" (Psalm l:1).

Always make prayer your first step in achieving any goal, for He can guide you along the way. Where you want to be guided may not be where He wants to guide you, which reminds me of the time when I purchased my first car.

After the Lord had blessed me with a new job, I needed a car to commute to and from work. Therefore, getting a car suddenly became one of my goals. I prayed and asked the Lord to help me to buy a car, and He supplied my need. However, before He did, I stayed before the Lord in prayer, for the enemy has his way of trying to deceive us to redirect our paths.

One day I stopped to look at some cars at a car dealer's lot and found one that seemed most interesting. I conveyed my interest to a salesman and initiated the transactions to purchase the car.

To my dismay, when I returned to complete the transaction and to pick up the car, the dealer didn't have the car ready. When I inquired about the car's condition, the salesman and dealer became very indignant, which made me think that something seemed peculiar. Nevertheless, I still wanted to purchase the car.

While I was standing there, the Holy Spirit told me not to pursue the matter and to walk away. "Walk away!" I thought to myself, "I have my money; I'm ready to buy this car; and I need it now."

Despite my desperation, anger, and disappointment, I knew that I had to be obedient. Furthermore, the Lord knows best for us.

Therefore, I was obedient and finally realized that it was not God's will that I purchase the car. As I was walking away, the Holy Spirit told me that there was another car for me.

I continued to pray, and the following week I searched in the *Boston Globe* and saw a car that I was interested in. I immediately called the owner, Diane, a very friendly young lady.

Although Diane was very congenial, as I conversed with her, I learned that she did not believe in Christ. However, after selling me her car, she shared a story with me about how she didn't feel right selling her car to others who had already seen it. She mentioned that her mind kept telling her not to sell the car to them.

After the transaction, I was witnessing to her about the Lord. I kept sharing stories of the Lord's goodness, hoping, too, that she would accept the Lord as her personal Saviour. Diane would listen attentively, but later would utter statements that implied that she was not ready to accept the Lord.

Well, one day I received a call from her. She told me that while she was on a minivacation, she decided to gather in an outdoor setting with some Christians who also talked to her about Christ. She told me that when an invitation was made to Christian discipleship, she went forth and accepted the Lord as her personal Saviour and now wanted to be baptized.

I was very happy for Diane as I knew that all the angels in heaven were rejoicing that a soul came to Christ. I continued to share Scriptures with her to help her in her new Christian walk as I relied upon the Holy Spirit to help me answer many of her questions. She was later baptized at the church I attend, Christ Temple Church of Personal Experience in Roxbury, Massachusetts.

That's how the Lord works. He uses someone to plant, another to water, but it is He Who gives the increase, drawing men to Himself. He drew Diane to Himself as He allowed us to lift up His name.

The Lord is good, and when we let Him into our lives, miraculous and beautiful things begin to happen. Not only did the Lord guide me in my car search, but in the process, He saved a soul.

Diane later mentioned to me that when she first accepted the Lord as her Saviour, many wonderful things immediately began to happen to her. She told me of the call that she had received from her estranged brother, whom she hadn't seen in years. She said that the Lord mended their relationship and they were friends again. Other good news included a new friend that came into her life, whom she later married.

God knows much more about our needs than we ourselves and guides us accordingly; I wanted the first car, but He said no. He always gets the final word. If what you are praying for is not within His will, He has His way of changing your desire to what He desires, which also recalls another experience to my mind.

I can remember when I wanted to write my first book, a novel portraying a character who went from rags to riches. Since I wanted the novel to appeal to a large audience, I felt that I had to create scenes about crimes, violence, fire, and deaths. I even had the nerve to ask the Lord to help me write it.

Because I kept seeking God's guidance, I slowly began to see my desire to write such a book diminish until it was completely gone. Later He made me understand why the desire wasn't fulfilled and changed that desire to one that would glorify Him. Through my spiritual growth, this changed desire resulted in this first writing: *Stepping Out on Faith.*

God knows best; all we need to do is to trust Him. "Trust in the Lord with all thine heart; and lean not to thine own understanding. In all thy ways acknowledge him, and he shall direct thy paths" (Prov. 3:5–6).

He is our Great Director. When He begins to lead you and direct you, lean not to your own understanding. Trust that the Lord is working things out for your good, as a result of your prayers.

How Shall We Pray

Throughout the *Holy Bible,* the Lord tells us when and how to pray. He doesn't leave us without answers. "And he spake a parable unto them to this end, that men ought always to pray, and not to faint" (Luke 18:1).

According to this Scripture, you should pray all the time. This means any time and anywhere: in the bathroom, kitchen, car, office, as you walk down the street, when you're talking to others and so forth. All of this does not require us to open our mouths; some takes the form of meditation. Our meditation upon Him can also be considered as our prayers—any way that our minds can reach God's.

Pour out your heart to God in prayer. As you talk to Him, you can talk to Him as you would a friend.

One of the most profound Scriptures concerning prayer that is found in the *Holy Bible* tells us that we should first pray, believing that we have that which we are asking of God. "What things soever ye desire, when ye pray, believe that ye receive them, and ye shall have them" (Mark 11:24). Believe that God has already granted your request, be patient, and wait for Him to deliver.

I don't know your goal or purpose in life, but when you pray, do as the Lord tells you: believe that you already have what you are praying for and claim it in His name. Picture yourself doing or having that which you are asking of God.

Visualization can be very helpful as I've exercised it in my own life. One experience that I can immediately recall is a story regarding my first newspaper reporting assignment. My background was in technical writing, but I also desired to work as a reporter.

After praying about obtaining a writing assignment, I began visualizing myself being a reporter, going in front of the mirror to practice the part. I didn't, however, just make the statement before the mirror; I had to put my faith in action.

One day, I telephoned a major local community newspaper and explained my desire and background. After the conversation, I was very happy to receive my first newspaper assignment.

Because the managing editor liked my first article, I was later given numerous writing assignments, allowing me to learn much more about people, community affairs, and issues. I feel that I obtained the job because I prayed and asked God for it. In addition, I believed that He had already granted the job to me before I actually received it.

One of Rev. Jessie Jackson's favorite statements: "If your mind can conceive it, your heart can believe it, then you can achieve it." Your achievement is dependent upon how much you can believe. Believe a little, get a little. Believe much, get much as a reward of your faith. Faith is crucial if you want God to answer your prayers, despite how you pray.

Relative to how to pray, the Lord tells us: "And when thou prayest, thou shalt not be as the hypocrites are: for they love to pray standing in the synagogues and in the corners of the streets, that they may be seen of men" (Matt. 6:5). The Scripture holds a strong message: never pray to be seen; your prayer is between you and God. He does not want you to be concerned about who is watching you when you pray.

Jesus told His disciples that praying to be seen is what hypocrites do, and: "Verily I say unto you, they have their reward." To those believers who want their prayers to be answered, He instructs: "But thou, when thou prayest, enter into thy closet, and when thou hast shut thy door, pray to thy Father which is in secret; and thy Father which is in secret shall reward thee openly. But when ye pray, use not vain repetitions, as the heathen do: for they think that they shall be heard for their much speaking. Be not ye therefore like unto them: for your Father knoweth what things ye have need of, before ye ask him" (Matt. 6:6–8).

Take all of your concerns into your secret closet and commune with God. Your secret closet can be any quiet place where you can talk to God, welcoming His presence. The Scripture also says to refrain from repetition when you pray.

The Lord knows what you need before you ask Him. The Psalmist David attests to this and states: "For there is not a word in my tongue, but, lo, O Lord, thou knowest it altogether" (Psalm 139:4).

God knows our innermost thoughts and nothing is hidden from Him, so your prayers don't have to be repetitious ones. Long prayers filled with repetition do not impress the Lord or cause Him to hear you more than He would if you had fewer words.

The Lord hears the prayers of those who seek after righteousness and try to live godly; these are His children and set apart for Him. "But know that the Lord hath set apart him that is godly for himself: the Lord will hear when I call unto him" (Psalm 4:3).

When you pray in the manner He desires (believing that He has already granted your request; praying not to be seen; avoiding repetition; and seeking after righteousness), the Lord can grant your request. In addition, the Lord can perform great and wondrous acts through prayers.

Wondrous Acts Through Prayer

God is awesome, and He can work wonders for you as a result of your prayers. Since the beginning of time, God has performed countless wondrous acts for His people because of their prayers. Marvel over His supreme and supernatural power.

"Who can utter the mighty acts of the Lord? who can shew forth all his praise" (Psalm 106:2)? Even if the Lord gives us a thousand tongues, we are still incapable of praising Him enough for his might.

Your prayer can cause the Lord to temporarily suspend the laws of nature and cause something supernatural or a miracle to happen for you. He has many ways of providing you with answers to everything troubling or confronting you.

The Lord's ways are perfect "and his greatness is unsearchable" (Psalm 145:3). Because of His greatness, there is nothing concerning you that He is incapable of performing, which reminds me of how the Lord stepped in for my mother and worked things out for her because of her prayers.

My mother was very sick and didn't know what was wrong with her. She only knew that she was experiencing such immense dizziness that she could hardly walk. Staggering and screaming, she went to a doctor, who thought that she was only drunk. He made her return home without an examination—only his ludicrous opinion that only a drunk person would behave in such a manner.

After my mother returned home, she sat on her living room sofa, and prayed to the Lord for a healing and that the doctor would find out what was wrong with her. After praying, she found that she felt much better the following day.

Desiring to know what caused her illness, she returned to the hospital for an examination and later found that tests showed that she had a cyst in her side that was larger than an egg. Because of the diagnosis, her doctor wanted to admit her to the hospital immediately to be operated on the following day.

However, since my mother was not experiencing any pain, she told her doctor that she wanted to return home first. She also stated that she would return to the hospital the next day for admission.

Upon her return to the hospital the following day, my mother stated that nine doctors stood around her bedside in the examination room, pushing and probing, trying to find the cyst.

Stunned and without any evidence of the cyst, one of the doctors told her, "Mrs. Spann, all I can say is that a miracle occurred. Your operation was scheduled at 5:00 A.M., but as far as I'm concerned you can be released at that time to go home."

God had stepped in and answered my mother's prayers and removed the cyst before her scheduled operation. Prayer does work wonders to bring about healing or any other wondrous act to help you achieve your goal.

Always pray about your goals. If you pray with faith, before you know it, you may be walking into all kinds of help and opportunities.

Your help may come in the form of an unexpected telephone call with nothing but good news, or a letter in your mail box with information that you needed a long time ago. You may be guided to someone who has already gone through what you are about to go through.

Where there is help take advantage of it. God is our help; don't forget to pray and cause your blessings to pass you by.

5

Believing in Yourself

"I can do all things through Christ which strengtheneth me" (Phil. 4:13).

A prerequisite for accomplishing your goal is to believe in yourself. You must believe in your God–given abilities. The more you believe in yourself and your abilities, the more confident you become to actualize your goal.

Regardless of your age, race, educational background, or any socioeconomic condition, you can achieve your goal if you have the faith to believe.

Furthermore, "in all these things we are more than conquerors through him that loved us" (Rom. 8:37).

The *Holy Bible* gives you full assurance and teaches you to believe within your heart: "I can do all things through Christ which strengtheneth me" (Phil. 4:13). Make this Scripture your foundation in all things that you strive to achieve, and place no limitations on the heights that you can climb in Christ.

When you turn the situation over to the Lord, you are then guided by Him, and He begins to work through you. You do nothing through your own power or might. Jesus reminds us in His Word that "without me ye can do nothing" (John 15:5). With Him, you can do all things.

Believing that you can do all things through Christ enables you to be optimistic, build your confidence, develop your ideas, and accept criticism.

Be Optimistic

If the Scripture says that "you can do all things through Christ," believe it, and be optimistic. You should have an optimistic view concerning your goal.

Optimism means that you are anticipating the best possible outcome for what you are trying to achieve. If one approach doesn't work, you are eager to try another and another until you get the job done. Keep trying until you are satisfied.

As often as possible, try never to allow negative thoughts to enter your mind, for "as a man thinks in his heart, so is he." Think negatively, and negative things happen. Think positively, and positive things happen.

For example, if you are studying to take a test but keep telling yourself that you won't be able to pass it, you probably won't. The negative cogitation sets you up for self–defeat, and it can also dictate how circumstances appear in your life. You just won't try as hard to pass because you already think that studying will be in vain.

On the other hand, when you use a positive approach and believe that you can pass the test, you begin to initiate whatever you feel is necessary to pass: you study harder and longer, hold study sessions with friends, or try your best to memorize facts. In essence, you become so determined to pass that you begin to employ any legitimate technique that you feel can help you.

Try to maintain positive thoughts and a positive outlook on life if you want to succeed at what you are trying to accomplish. Fellowshipping with other Christians can also help you to stay focused; surround yourself by them. Sometimes this happens to us subconsciously because like spirits attract each other. Good is attracted to good, and evil is attracted to its kind.

One who strives to be a true Christian tries to hold a positive outlook on life and bases his decisions and actions on godly principles. There is no guarantee that others will hold your exact views concerning a particular situation, but they may be able to offer other positive approaches that can be beneficial to you.

> Regardless of your age, race, educational background, or any socioeconomic condition, you can achieve your goal if you have the faith to believe.

Sometimes it is advantageous to look at a situation from someone else's point of view. When we are too close to a situation, we can become blinded to other positive possibilities.

Your mind must be constantly occupied with positive thoughts, even if you have to keep encouraging and motivating yourself. Fellowshipping with other believers can help motivate you, but allowing yourself to be totally dependent upon any person ignores what the Lord wants for you. In addition, the Lord wants us to trust and depend on Him. When we do and when others are no longer around to encourage us, He is still there to lead us.

Even though you do not know the road that will lead you to accomplish your goal, be optimistic about the One Who is guiding you to make it happen. If you are ready to be led, He is ready and willing to take you by the hand and lead you.

While you are being led, you will probably have your share of trials despite your optimism. When you encounter any trial, your success through it will have a lot to do with positive or negative thoughts that you hold. If you always magnify problems that you foresee down the road, your chances of starting the endeavor are lessened. You can anticipate future situations, but you do not have to let them become roadblocks.

Try to put the situation in proper perspective and "cross each bridge" when you encounter it. Take one day at a time with a positive attitude. Begin your day thanking the Lord for the day that He has made. Thank Him and believe that it is going to be a good day and that something good awaits you. Remember, success and pessimism don't mix.

Pessimism is an inclination to emphasize adverse aspects, conditions, and possibilities. In other words, if you are a pessimistic person and hold negative views, you are more inclined to expect the worst possible outcome concerning what you aspire to accomplish. Your attitude, which usually results from how you feel toward a state or fact, very often determines your behavior.

The best way to avoid pessimism and become optimistic is to entrust what you are trying to achieve to God. Therefore, "Commit thy works unto the Lord, and thy thoughts shall be established" (Prov. 16:3). There is no failure in Him, so you can be optimistic that what you feel the Lord is inspiring you to do is going to be successful. If you fail, it may mean that you have stopped seeking advice from the Lord or that you did not wait patiently on Him.

In your optimism, always look beyond your problems, for "all things work together for good to them that love God, to them who are the called according to his purpose" (Rom. 8:28). Try to learn something from each experience. That lesson can ultimately make you stronger and help to prepare you for your next step or experience.

If your first experience was unsuccessful, try it again. This is where persistence and determination are essential. When you are highly determined to achieve a task, you become persistent in your effort to actualize it. This may mean doing it repeatedly until you get it right.

It doesn't mean, however, making the same mistakes repeatedly. Learn from those mistakes, and try to research and implement a new way to do the task if necessary.

One of my philosophies concerning attaining any goal is that God is always willing to help those who are willing to help themselves, but you must first put forth your best effort. Sometimes doing your best requires a lot of hard work. To some, hard work seems to be bad news. The good news, however, is that the joy of having achieved a task always exceeds what you considered hard work.

If you want to succeed at anything, learn how to be optimistic. Find a positive message in all of your experiences. For example, you may have just lost your job. Hold on—it may not not be as bad as you may perceive. Don't view losing your job as failure. Look at it from a positive perspective.

Your lost job allows more time for you to chart a new path. With your job, you couldn't take much time to do this. In essence, you can create a new beginning for yourself. In the process, create for yourself a new attitude. If you have been doing well in your last position, think of how you can do things even better when you find another job or decide to start a business of your own.

Just remember, there is always a good message in everything that faces you if you love the Lord and have given your life completely over to Him.

Your positive attitude can help you to chart a successful path to reach your goal, so flush out all negative thoughts. Fill your mind daily with fresh, new creative thoughts of faith, love, and goodness.

In fact, the Apostle Paul gives us direct instructions on what should occupy our minds: "whatsoever things are true, whatsoever things are honest, whatsoever things are just, whatsoever things are pure, whatsoever things are lovely, whatsoever things are of a good report; if there be any virtue, and if there be any praise, think on these things" (Phil. 4:8).

Build Your Confidence

Confidence means the quality or state of being certain. When you exert confidence in your abilities, you have a greater chance of convincing yourself and others that you can accomplish your endeavor.

There are many situations that you can encounter that require you to be able to convince others of your abilities. Of course, to convince others of your abilities, you must first believe in them yourself.

If you are not confident in the abilities that you possess, there are ways that you can build your confidence. First and foremost to building your confidence is to pray and ask God for more confidence in the abilities that He has given you.

He does not withhold any good thing from anyone who asks of Him. "But let him ask in faith, nothing wavering. For he that wavereth is like a wave of the sea driven with the wind and tossed" (James 1:6).

Don't doubt the Lord's ability to supply you with confidence or any skill that you feel you lack for your success. Try testing your faith in God by asking Him to do one small thing at a time.

When He brings it to pass, try your faith again and ask Him to perform a task that you consider to be a little harder than the first. When you try your faith, you'll find that your faith and confidence in God increases each time He answers your request.

Try it today. Pray to God and ask Him to bring a very small task to pass. Believe sincerely as you pray that He is going to do this for you. Wait for Him to deliver.

Don't forget that our time is not God's time. Therefore, you may not receive an answer immediately, but when you are patient with Him, He answers right on time. When He does (and He will if your prayer was one of faith), thank Him and praise Him for His work. Let others know what you have asked the Lord to do for you and how He has answered your prayers.

This process of telling others of the Lord's goodness is called testifying. Testify as often as you can and give God thanks for all He has done. "A thankful heart receives much." Now, when He sees that you are thankful, He becomes even more generous the next time you go to Him in prayer to ask Him to perform another task.

In addition to prayer, another way to build your confidence is to enhance your skills. Continue your education. This doesn't necessarily require enrolling in a class, which can be expensive. Read books, newspapers, and newsletters; listen and talk to mentors; or use other self-educational approaches.

If you are searching for a job or considering a career change, read the book, *What Color is Your Parachute* by Richard Bolles. Research ways to enhance your skills to build your confidence.

When you exhibit confidence, you can move ahead to develop your ideas.

Develop Your Idea

Never shun an idea (or task) because you feel it was never done before; if you feel that it is inspired by God, take time to develop it. Anything ever accomplished in life derived from a single idea. Many of our ideas are criticized and ridiculed before they ever begin to prove true and valuable. Don't put yours aside.

Imagine how Alexander Graham Bell must have felt when he wanted to invent the telephone. In the early days, Bell's idea must have seemed ridiculous to a great number of people. His family, friends, and colleagues laughed at him because he told them his idea of transmitting the sound of voice through wire.

Nevertheless, Bell pursued his dream against enormous odds. If he had stopped and become discouraged at the responses from others who were told of his venture, the world may not have known such a remarkable thing called the telephone.

Consequently, before the telephone became such a phenomenal success, one person took a risk with himself and his reputation to develop an idea. Take a look around you. All those vehicles, machinery, equipment, and other man-made things were invented and developed through many ideas—usually starting from just one person's idea.

Because you may feel you are the "first" in your endeavor, don't be afraid of developing your idea. It took many "firsts" to build this nation to the country that it is today. Because the pilgrims were tired of being subjected to their country's laws, which had no respect for religious freedom, they had an idea to travel to a strange land where they could worship the Lord any way they desired. They ventured out on a journey they hadn't taken before. We know that land today as America.

In many ways, you must be like the pilgrims; take a chance on travelling down an unknown road to reach your goal, if necessary. The journey, however, doesn't have to be a lonely one. But once you have accepted the Lord as your personal Saviour, you never have to worry about walking alone. You can face every situation boldly, knowing that the Lord is right by your side—your Partner, Who promises never to leave you.

> Many of our ideas are criticized and ridiculed before they ever begin to prove true and valuable. Don't put yours aside.

Your Partner gives all the instructions and directions, and all you have to do is follow. Practice sharing everything with Him. Talk to Him as you would talk to a friend. You will find that He not only listens, but also gives you answers that He feels are best for you. The Lord wants to be your Best Friend. Of course, He can touch your natural friends to be there for you as well.

If you are inspired to do something in a new way, go ahead and be a pioneer if you feel that the Lord is instructing you to do it. If you need to sharpen or hone your skills to accomplish the task, do so. As you implement your plans, don't let criticism, which is sure to surface, hinder you.

Accept Criticism

Are you convinced that you can accomplish the goal that you have set out to achieve? Are you also ready and willing to stand up for what you really believe in? I hope that you can honestly answer yes to these questions.

You must hold steadfast (at all times) to your beliefs because once you set out to achieve your goal, your critics will also be at work. They may criticize you constructively and destructively. Learn to distinguish between the two.

Constructive criticism can yield good results. It can make something that is good even better. Anyone who offers constructive criticism wants to help you and see you move ahead to accomplish your goal.

Be aware also that constructive criticism can also hurt despite how good a person's intent to help you may be. The truth will stand, but hearing it may be painful. Regardless of how painful, try to accept it without getting angry in the process.

When constructive criticism hurts, you may be very tempted to question the person's motives for giving you certain advice. Learn how to put your sensitivity behind you and accept advice that can help you.

Constructive criticism is not to be regarded negatively. It is not a personal attack on you. To help you tell whether advice others give you is intended for your best interest, ask yourself some of these questions:

- Is the advice helpful and given in a manner to improve upon the situation instead of to insult or discourage?

  The manner in which someone says something to you makes a big difference in its ability to help you, regardless of how constructive the criticism may be.

- Does the person comment on good points first, indicate what is wrong next, and then offer advice on how to improve the matter?

  Often, just telling someone what he has done wrong is not too constructive or helpful. The critic should also provide suggestions that can improve the situation.

When you cannot answer yes to these questions, try to avoid the advice. The criticism can be considered destructive and targeted to destroy any chance of your successfully accomplishing your goal.

Destructive criticism is harmful, and you should disregard the advice. A person who criticizes destructively does not want to see good in anything that you do. Therefore, he has nothing good to say to you and repeatedly finds faults in what you do. The more you try to improve a situation per his suggestions, the more faults the critic finds. His intention is evil and malicious.

I strongly feel that people who give destructive criticism purposely are not trying to follow the ways of the Lord. I try my best to avoid them, for the Holy Scripture says: "Blessed is the man that walketh not in the counsel of the ungodly" (Psalm 1:1). When you avoid their advice, consider yourself blessed by God.

There is no good in destructive criticism. People who criticize in a destructive manner usually make such statements as:

> "You can't do it, no matter how hard you try."
>
> "Just face it; some people are destined to be winners while others are destined to be losers. You were born to be a loser. You have never achieved anything good in your life."

> "Save yourself all the trouble. What you are trying to do has never been done before. You should stop wasting your time because time is precious."
>
> "You need to have a formal education to do that and you should have a 4–year college degree."
>
> While some professions do require proper preparation with college studies, not all do. If more preparation is required for what you want to do, who says that you cannot prepare yourself?

If you find that you have been listening to those who continuously give you wrong or negative advice intentionally, you don't have to any longer. When your critic tells you again that you can't achieve a particular goal, don't be afraid to say: "You are right; I can't, but God can. If He wants to use me to accomplish it, if I were you, I wouldn't try to stand in His way." This will silence your critic, for surely if God is for you, He is more than the whole world against you.

Keep God on your side, ignore destructive criticism, and go ahead and initiate your goal, for starting is already half the battle. Once you have started, keep moving up, looking to the Lord, and you won't become discouraged along the way. Remember, you only have one-half the way left before finishing.

There is no time to be discouraged. It may seem that the harder you try, someone is always waiting to knock you down, "for the wicked are quick to run and do mischief." What you thought would be easy turns out to be another battle. If this is so, don't quit because a quitter never wins.

"Have you not known or have you not heard that the Lord will fight your battle?" Who or what negative circumstance can fight against God? Remember the enemy is a defeated foe through the name of Jesus Christ.

Allow people who criticize constructively to help you, and always try to avoid those who criticize destructively.

6

Trusting God To Make a Way

"Is any thing too hard for the Lord" (Gen. 18:14)?

Desiring to accomplish a task that ultimately blesses others is one of the primary focuses of Christianity. Your desire, however, to achieve and to become a channel in which others can be blessed is only the beginning and accomplishing it may not be easy.

As you begin to work, you can quickly become conscious of difficulties and problems in your way. These problems can either threaten or hinder you from reaching your goal.

Despite forms in which they are presented, you can rise above obstacles because God can make a way for those who trust Him. Your faith in Him helps you to triumph over all situations that confront you. Furthermore, you can face these circumstances and ask boldly: "Is anything too hard for the Lord" (Gen. 18:14)?

Because you are convinced that nothing is too hard for God, you can rise above your circumstances and be patient and wait on Him.

Rise Above Your Circumstances

Your problems can come to you in streams and in countless forms. They can be seen as your tough times, but be confident that you can rise above circumstances that you face.

The lack of money can be one of your toughest problems. It can threaten you and prevent you from stepping out to do what you want to accomplish. The lack of money can also cause you to put your plan on hold indefinitely.

However, amid any financial crisis, there is always hope. You don't have to panic when your finances are inadequate for your needs, for "where there's a will, there's a way." The story about Mary McLeod Bethune fascinates me of this fact.

Bethune was a black woman born to poverty, who gave her life to the Lord at a very young age. After the Lord answered her prayer to learn how to read and write, she later desired to share her knowledge with others in a school of her own despite her lack of money.

With only $1.50, she opened a school with her son and five little girls. Her school was a 1–room cottage. She used a packing crate for her desk and boxes for her students' chairs.

Giving thanks and glorifying God, Bethune opened and marched into her school singing "Leaning on the Everlasting Arms" and later reciting the 23rd Psalm. Since that opening day, her school grew tremendously and later merged with another school to become Bethune–Cookman College, a 4–year institution in Florida that educates thousands.

Bethune's story helps to convey how the Lord can help you reach your goal despite your lack of finances. Be willing to use your creativity.

I find that if you look at your goal as a whole, its costs of implementation can sometimes seem overwhelming. If you treat it in parts, financing one part at a time can be more manageable, less expensive, and more attainable.

> They can be seen as your tough times, but be confident that you can rise above circumstances that you face.

Take one milestone at a time, brainstorm your ideas, and note various ways that you can acquire money that you need to accomplish that milestone. In your brainstorming, try not to omit any possibilities. When you're through brainstorming, go through your list and maintain only the approaches that are reasonable.

Set out to accomplish that milestone. After accomplishing it, repeat the process for each milestone until you have accomplished all of them.

Outside of my regular job, I've done free–lance writing and have even sold encyclopedias. Granted, I never developed a love for selling encyclopedias. But selling them didn't really bother me because I believe that the product is an excellent research tool. In addition, selling the encyclopedias was a means to an end. Apparently, selling them did upset a friend whom I once dated. For whatever reason, he didn't like one of my advertising approaches: placing fliers in selected business locales to attract customers.

One day, my friend came across one of my fliers. On the flier, I had listed my home telephone number and purposely omitted my name. He later telephoned me and spilled his outrage, accusing me of putting my telephone number all across town. His accusation didn't hinder me or cause me to retrieve my fliers because I knew my mission and couldn't afford to let his pettiness interfere.

Perhaps you, too, will be confronted by someone who opposes your method or effort to increase your financial base. If you are not firm in your belief, you may be sidetracked. In your creativity for discovering ways to satisfy your financial needs, if what you finally choose does not conflict with God's law, go for it!

When finance is not your hindrance, sometimes just being afraid or unknowledgeable about devising a plan keeps you idle. It doesn't have to; network and talk to others. You will find that people love sharing information. Communicating with others can also help you avoid mistakes that others have made. Don't try to recreate the wheels. Find out the basics and build upon them.

In addition, your circumstance may be that everything seems to be going wrong all at once, making it harder and harder for you to realize your goal. "When it rains, it pours." This is a familiar cliche, which may seem true in many situations. However, your faith in God enables you to believe that "the rain eventually stops, and behind every dark cloud, the sun shines."

Amid a stream of these unanticipated circumstances that may surround you, don't become dismayed and let go of your faith. If God has entrusted you with a specific work,

He will also make a way for you to achieve it. His help does not come automatically. You have to always trust and rely on Him to lead you.

Despite the circumstance that is threatening to hinder you from attaining your goal, there is nothing too hard for God. If you need a financial blessing, job, healing (physically or emotionally), a marriage to be saved, whatever the problem, He can solve it. Take everything that you are going through to Him in prayer, leave it there, and walk away with a victory.

The Lord is truly amazing and can do exceedingly far above all you can ask or think. Appropriate words cannot describe His wonders; He takes pleasure in making a way for His children, for He loves and cares for them.

This reminds me of how I obtained my current job. The job that I wanted was at a company located approximately 1 hour away from my home. I didn't have a car to commute to and from work, and I couldn't get there by public transportation.

When I was interviewed for the job, I had to ask family members and others to drive me to the company. As we travelled, I can recall being asked, "Shirley, if you get the job, how are you going to get to work each day?"

I had to answer honestly. I told them that I didn't know and that I was believing God to make a way for me. The Lord was my only hope.

"The Lord will make a way for you," were favorite words of my grandmother, who died in 1991. She always used to tell me, "Shirley, don't worry about not having a car to get to work. You concentrate on getting the job first. With the Lord's help, you'll get to the job."

In essence, she was telling me to take one step at a time, and believe in the Lord to supply my needs. Her strong faith that somehow the Lord would supply my needs helped to strengthen my faith. She uttered her statement with such strong conviction that from that moment on, I really began to exercise and apply that kind of faith in my life.

Well, I had decided to take one day at a time. First, I started believing that the Lord would supply the job, and He did. After He had blessed me with the job, I then began believing that He would provide a way for me to commute to and from work.

I was inspired to give my new employer a starting date that would allow me ample time to find transportation. Several thoughts entered my mind on how to proceed to resolve my transportation situation. However, calling the company to inquire about a van pool was one thought that seemed heaviest on my mind and most emphatic.

Therefore, I called the company. I stayed on the telephone practically all day, making numerous telephone calls determined to find transportation. In one of my conversations, I was finally informed that a van pool was leaving near my area. I telephoned the driver and informed him of my situation, and he stated that he had a seat available on his van.

Just as I believed Him to make a way for me, He did. The van became my ride to and from work each day until I was able to get a car.

Today, I still thank God for providing me with the job and making a way for me to get there. I kept praying for Him to make a way for me, believed that He would, and stepped out on my faith. In other words, I had to put my faith to work.

As mentioned earlier, in order for our faith to be justified, it must be accompanied by our works. Take a step to do what you want to achieve and believe that the Lord is stepping along side of you. Don't defeat yourself with negative thoughts before you try. Step out on faith.

If I had told myself, "Well, I shouldn't bother trying to get the job since I don't have a car," I wouldn't have gotten the job or the ride. Instead, I decided to turn the situation over to the Lord and moved according to His directions.

You can rise above any of your circumstances by believing that the Lord will make a way for you to help you achieve your desire. We serve such a wonderful God, Who is ready and willing to help us at any time. All He requires of us is that we live as He commands and believe that He is going to bring what we ask of Him to pass.

Trying to understand how He works is irrelevant, for His ways are unsearchable. He is sovereign and has all powers in His hand to do what He wants to do when He wants to do it.

Learn to call on the Lord and be patient and wait on Him, even as you utilize energy and imagination given to you by Him.

Be Patient and Wait

Does it ever appear to you that everyone is always in a rush? No one wants to wait. Waiting requires patience, and many of us just aren't patient.

For example, when some of us visit the bank or supermarket, the first thing that usually appalls us is having to wait in long lines for service. And, of course, we feel that our service is always the most urgent. Immediately our eyes begin to gaze across the room for shorter lines. To our dismay, all other lines appear even longer. What do we do then?

The ones who are patient remain in line, while others who are impatient vacate it to go elsewhere for service, hoping to avoid the waiting period. After the impatient person arrives at his destination, surprised and disappointed, he finds even longer lines than before. As unfair as many of us may feel it is, sometimes we just have to be patient and wait.

Patience is an invaluable asset. With it, you don't complain unnecessarily. You remain steadfast despite difficulty, opposition, or adversity. It is essential that you learn to be patient and wait, especially if you want God to move in your behalf.

If you are convinced that God will make a way for you to help you achieve your goal, be patient and wait for Him to do so. Sometimes we pray earnestly for God to bless us and seldomly want to wait. When He is ready to bless us, we have forgotten about our prayers and tried to take matters into our own hands.

Our blessings must not only be uttered in prayers, but they must also be waited for and received in prayer. No one knows when God will move; He sets an appointed time to come to our rescue.

It is essential that you learn to be patient and wait, especially if you want God to move in your behalf.

You may feel that a lot of time is elapsing and you are not seeing any result. Continue waiting; He never forgets about you. When you least expect it, the Lord begins to pour out your blessings where you won't even have enough room to store them.

Have you ever prayed for a job, began your search, and then waited for God to supply it? When He did answer, not only did one company offer you a job, but you also had others calling at the same time to offer you work.

Surely, this was more work than you could have performed. Since you couldn't obviously perform all of them, you had to decline offers. In our patience, God provides so many blessings that we can't accept all of them because there is no more room to store them.

Pray and wait, for God can do great things even in the midst of your waiting. As you wait, He can cause you to encounter certain situations that ultimately help you to grow spiritually. In your growth, you can become a stronger person with more understanding of His might, allowing you to rise to where He wants you to be.

As the Scripture commands, "Wait on the Lord: be of good courage, and he shall strengthen thine heart: wait, I say, on the Lord" (Psalm 27:14). When you wait, He can make a way for you.

I love to hear my mother's testimonies of God's capacity to make a way for His children and how He always makes a way for her. My mother stated that one day my grandmother called and told her that she needed some money by a certain date. My mother didn't have much money at the time, but she knew that she had to try her best to help her mother. Therefore, she assured my grandmother that the money would be there.

My mother also mentioned that as soon as she hung up the telephone, one of her brothers telephoned and stated that he also needed some money and wanted to know if she could help in any way. Again, my mother assured him that she would do what she could to help.

After the telephone calls, my mother sent all the money that she had, not leaving any for herself to get through the following work week. After denying herself, she prayed and asked God to supply her needs, and He did.

On the following day, my mother went to work and found money lying on the floor. She told her supervisor about the money that she had found, and he told her that he could not trace the money to its owner. Because of this, he stated that she could keep the money. My mother said that the money was more than sufficient to sustain her for the week, plus the next.

In addition, my mother went with one of her friends later during that same week to another company to apply for work because she thought she needed another job. She was hired and was to start her new job the following Monday, but she became ill that Friday night and went to the hospital.

After examining her, the doctor told my mother that she needed an operation. Wanting to avoid being operated on, she prayed to God and asked for healing. Upon returning to the hospital, and being re–examined, the doctor informed her that she didn't need the operation. My mother knew then that the Lord had heard her prayers.

After the Lord had healed her, my mother was able to go to her new part–time job on Monday night. To her surprise, her supervisor handed her a paycheck on her first night! Appearing perplexed, she told him that she didn't work the previous week and that particular night was her first night on the job.

Her supervisor asked her, "Did you write your name on the check?" My mother answered, "No." He replied, "I didn't, so the check is yours." My mother said that she was stunned, accepted the check, and looked up to heaven and said, "What a mighty God we serve!" She also told me that she knew God would make a way, and He did. Praise God, for He is the Provider!

The Lord moved miraculously in my mother's behalf because she believed that He would make a way for Her. I'm also reminded of a testimony that my Bible study teacher once shared in a class one evening of how God makes a way for His own.

He told us that it was between semesters when he had a great need for money to buy his school books. He said that he had promised himself that he wouldn't write home to his father asking for money because he felt that his father was already trying to help him the best that he could. He said that he prayed that the Lord would make a way for him.

It was now Friday, and Monday seemed to have been getting closer and closer. He didn't have the first book to begin class and didn't know where he would get the money. He stated that he kept believing that the Lord would answer his prayer.

Believing the Lord to answer his prayer, He mentioned that somehow he was led to go to the mail room. He looked in his mail box and found a letter, which was sent from his Aunt Bea. He stated that he had never received a letter from her in his life and wondered if something had happened. He opened the letter, and there was a check in it for $25.

He started smiling and said that in 1957, $25 was an enormous amount of money. His aunt had stated in her letter that she had read in the newspaper that college students were struggling financially around that time of year and felt she wanted to help him along.

He mentioned that her help was more than sufficient, since books in those days cost between $2 and $3. He suddenly found that he had enough money for all the books that he needed with some extra spending money left.

As illustrated in these testimonies, God will make a way for all those who put their trust in Him. Why not trust Him today to help you achieve your goal?

7

Pleasing God

"...be rich in good works, ready to distribute, willing to communicate; Laying up in store for themselves a good foundation against the time to come, that they may lay hold on eternal life" (I Tim. 6:18–19).

Always seek to please God in what you strive to achieve. God is Alpha and Omega, the Beginning and the End, allowing you to achieve all your goals through Jesus Christ.

Though many points are discussed in this book to help you achieve your goals, the fundamental principle that it seeks to convey is that you can do all things through Christ.

This, however, requires faith in God, for "without faith it is impossible to please him: for he that cometh to God must believe that he is, and that he is a rewarder of them that diligently seek him" (Heb. 11:6).

In your climb to reach your God–inspired goal, never try to please man to gain the riches of the world. "But thou, O man of God, flee these things; and follow after righteousness, godliness, faith, love, patience, meekness" (I Tim. 6:11). Therefore, put God first.

Always put God first as the Scripture commands. "But seek ye first the kingdom of God, and his righteousness; and all these things shall be added unto you" (Matt. 6:33).

Consider your goal as one of those "things" as mentioned in the Scripture and be optimistic that the Lord will grant it to you if you put Him first in your life. Putting Him first requires studying His holy Word to learn of Him and applying His laws and principles to your daily life.

When you put God first, He promises to make your way prosperous. "This book of the law shall not depart out of thy mouth; but thou shalt meditate therein day and night, that thou mayest observe to do according to all that is written therein: for then thou shalt make thy way prosperous, and then thou shalt have good success" (Josh. 1:8). The Scripture holds a blessed promise; all you need to do is put Him first in all things, drawing and attracting positive conditions around you.

Set aside anything that you feel is a top priority in your life, and put God first.

When you don't make pleasing God your first priority, those things that you regard more highly than Him can cause you to lose your soul. "For what shall it profit a man, if he shall gain the whole world, and lose his own soul" (Mark 8:36)?

The Apostle Paul encourages us in his epistle that we should not "trust in uncertain riches, but in the living God, who giveth us richly all things to enjoy" (I Tim 6:17). Unfortunately, many people advocate that the Lord wants His children to be poor.

I disagree, for how can you help someone if you don't have what he needs? One without food cannot satisfy another's hunger or quench another's thirst by drawing water from an empty well. The Lord gives us richly all things to enjoy and to help each other. However, He does not want us to put our trust in these uncertain riches.

He charges ministers entrusted with the gospel that they tell the believers to "do good, that they be rich in good works, ready to distribute, willing to communicate; Laying up in store for themselves a good foundation against the time to come, that they may lay hold on eternal life" (I Tim. 6:18–19).

> "But seek ye first the kingdom of God, and his righteousness; and all these things shall be added unto you" (Matt. 6:33).

I pray that you seek to please God with what you are trying to achieve so that He is glorified. "Thou art worthy, O Lord, to receive glory and honour and power: for thou hast created all things, and for thy pleasure they are and were created" (Rev. 4:11).

Therefore, always delight to do His will as the Psalmist David: "I delight to do thy will, Oh my God"

(Psalm 40:8), and He shall surely give thee the desires of your heart.

Step out on faith to reach your goal. With God, nothing shall be impossible, enabling you to do all things through Jesus Christ.